Preface

This special AR monograph considers the work of Andrew Bromberg of Aedas through the extraordinary prism of The Star in Singapore, which splices together shopping, socialising, culture and performance to create a new kind of armature for urban activities. Beyond the uninhibited drama of its architecture, The Star also reconceptualises the notion of public space for the tropics, rejecting the default template of the air-conditioned mall in favour of a sheltered, naturally ventilated inside/outside space that changes character through the day and is animated by a constant flow of visitors. In this, as in other projects, Bromberg's achievement reconnects people with place, transforming the tabula rasa of a suburban site into an intense and lively focus for social engagement. By seeing things differently, coupled with a design intelligence honed by the worldwide demand for quantity and speed, he succeeds in synthesising an architecture of spectacle that is more nuanced, agile and responsive than its initial object quality might suggest.

Based in the firm's Hong Kong office, Bromberg is that rare thing, a recognisable presence and design hand within the impressively global Aedas network. As an operation that thrives on the challenges of delivering expertise and efficiency across a range of professional services, Aedas does not generally define itself by the work of a particular architect, but Bromberg is an exception, striving to make meaningful architecture in rapidly changing locales such as the Middle East and China, as well as addressing the expectations of a demanding client base. Beyond the compelling set piece of The Star, the quartet of projects also shown here epitomises the depth and diversity of his work. Yet as the American critic Joseph Giovannini has noted, as a Western architect confronted with the scale and momentum of the Asian urban experience, Bromberg cannot simply rely on transplanting an inappropriate nostalgia for European attitudes and approaches. Though his division within Aedas is a comparatively modest operation, it is characterised by its capacity for experimentation and innovation, more think-tank than studio, energetically embracing and shaping the future.

Catherine Slessor, Editor, The Architectural Review

Introduction

Sutherland Lyall considers the creative and collaborative approach to practice of Andrew Bromberg and his Aedas studio

Given big-practice architects' preference for no-name anonymity, Andrew Bromberg's 50 or so strong unit in Aedas's Hong Kong office comes as a big surprise. He runs it as a fiefdom almost independent of one of the biggest practices in the world, which has nearly 2,000 people in 26 offices across the globe and 750 people in its Hong Kong office alone. At that scale you might reasonably expect something unusual in the way Aedas runs itself. But allowing a subset of a practice's corporate structure to develop its own separate legend is probably unique in the annals of world architecture which is not exactly known for its generosity in crediting fellow designers. We rarely hear about the whizzkid architects beavering in the studios of the current pantheon of starchitects unless, like the former Foster stalwart, Ken Shuttleworth, they finally break free to form their own practices. The Aedas surprise comes not only because Bromberg's practice-within-a-practice breaks the corporate rule of anonymity, but also because it successfully produces so many big commercial buildings. Mostly they are very big commercial buildings whose singularity of form suggests a happily wilful ignorance of the ritual gross-to-net mantras of developer clients.

Sometimes Bromberg designs – such as the 2005 plant-like Al Reem Island mixed-use design and the writhing clusters of the Bangkok corporate towers of 2006 – are almost whimsically organic. But the warped tower of the Ocean Heights development in Dubai of 2004-10, the twisted column of the 2006-11 U-Bora Tower in Dubai and the swooping folds of the Abu Dhabi Empire Tower of 2006-12 represent a massive command of stately form unknown in the West, and even the Middle East in which they stand. So too the 2007 design for Khor Dubai Wharfage whose raking component towers emerge like some lost giant saurian from the water's edge. At the same time The Star in Singapore, completed in 2012, is an intricate assemblage of props and masses which, like the 2010 Dance and Music Centre in The Hague, unexpectedly reference contemporaneous art experiments in Europe such as those of Rachel Whiteread.

These and the scores of others designed over the 10 years of the American Bromberg in Hong Kong are all vast projects, many of them the outcome of the competitions he enthusiastically entered from the beginning of his time in Asia. Apart from grudging admiration, the big question architects want to pose is precisely how he managed to hang on to most of his original design concepts.

Critic Aaron Betsky points out many of Bromberg's clients are less anonymous corporations than entrepreneurs 'who believe they can find value where others have not ... and believe they must create a product that is distinctive both in terms of how it appears and what it delivers in terms of space and amenities'. Right now such entrepreneurial developers seem to flourish in the Middle and Far East, a locus which Bromberg presciently identified at the very beginning of his career with Aedas and prompted his move to the Hong Kong office in 2000.

As with many commissions in these locales, The Star in Singapore reflects a scale of ambition and programmatic complexity that would be rare to find in an equivalent project in Europe or the USA. Not only a compelling object building, The Star is also an armature for different kinds of activities (shopping, eating, socialising, culture). Consciously rejecting the default template of a sealed and air-conditioned mall, The Star, with its naturally cooled retail atrium, thoughtfully reconceptualises the notion of public space for the modern tropical city in social, architectural and experiential terms. In doing so it provides a much-needed paradigm for similar developments, extending the lineage of tropical Modernism in a way that is both context and climate specific.

Bromberg is also aware of the power of gesture to anchor and animate the public realm. The Star has a formal exuberance that catalyses a new and rather nondescript suburban neighbourhood. Other recent projects such as the new West Kowloon Terminus in Hong Kong and an exhibition complex in Guangzhou are equally effective in electrifying their surroundings.

Architects are taught to design rationally and systematically: to research the brief and its special conditions, to test out, customarily with three-dimensional models, the possible arrangements of forms and masses and after a lot of thought and sketch designs finally to come up with a well reasoned solution. It rarely works that way in Bromberg's environment. Clients want rendered design drawings the next day – in one case in order to begin selling off-plan units the following week. In another he had three hours to make the initial design for a competition and a week to refine and revise it.

2. Model of an unbuilt competition proposal for a dance centre and school in The Hague. Studios for students and performers are separated by a canyon-like space

3. The dramatically sculptural volumes of the Empire Tower in Abu Dhabi. Layered towers alternately compress and flare

4. Bromberg's initial sketch of The Star which crystallised the architectural concept

5. The finished building is remarkably faithful to the original idea

6. Mixed-use complex at Al Reem Island in Abu Dhabi

7. Writhing towers linked by a skydeck in Bangkok reflect an Asian approach to scale

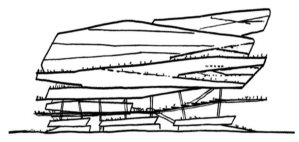

So in response to the demands of this new urgent market, Bromberg normally starts by producing a concept sketch, the Big Idea, to which he and his team make alterations, trying out a limited number of iterations as subsequent circumstances demand. But the original Big Idea essentially represents the core vision of the completed building. As one of the teams argues, 'I think you spend your time effectively by solving the problem instead of trying to consider countless ideas.' Here is a process which seems to lack the gravitas of lengthy preliminary research, but which is not inherently any riskier than the conventional Western approach to generating design solutions for clients. And it is of an order of magnitude faster.

Bromberg runs his team of young architects in, as he explains, 'a close family-like relationship'. It has the advantage of being able to access the expertise of everybody in the global practice. And it does this without losing its own identity. Individuals who join the team, most of them straight out of architecture school, are free to work on projects which excite them and they subsequently move around to expand their experience.

The Bromberg process is too a recognition that the headlong environment of current Asian commercial development operates by its own rules, not those of generations brought up in the West. And it recognises that architects have to work in the context of those conventions – which is to say very fast and with a sharp eye on cost.

Bromberg's skating precariously on the perimeter of developer convention is what makes his work so fascinating. And yet it is fundamentally conventional in accounting terms. He says, 'We live in the world where economic viability is always a priority. If you are going to build something that has never been seen before, it is your responsibility as the architect to make sure that the client can profit from it.'

Bromberg – and probably Aedas – takes the view that there may be a downside to having a star designer in the process of developing a brand of his own who has the right to choose his clients. But the upside is a single name, a face with which clients can identify. And although it is that of Andrew Bromberg, it is also Aedas itself. So that the design magic created by Bromberg is something which not only accumulates around his clients and his team, but also around the greater entity which is global Aedas.

8. Raking component towers emerge from the water's edge like a lost giant saurian at Khor Dubai

9. The recently completed CX 2-1 in Singapore provides a regional headquarters for one of the world's leading entertainment companies. The terraces will be eventually colonised by luxuriant greenery

10. The distinctive torqued tower at the Ocean Heights development in Dubai displays an assured command of stately form

11. A new exhibition complex on the edge of Guangzhou consists of two horizontal blocks, each with exhibition or retail spaces in a podium and offices or a hotel above

12. The U-Bora Tower in Dubai jousting with the Burj Khalifa's pinnacle

13. Conceived as a gateway to Hong Kong, the Express Rail Link West Kowloon Terminus is now under construction and is due to be completed in 2015. The visualisation does not reflect the future West Kowloon Cultural District located adjacent to the harbour

8

12

9

10

11

13

THE STAR

Beyond its role as a compelling and charismatic object building anchoring a still-evolving suburban landscape, The Star is a place both for people and the dynamics of modern spectacle

CRITICISM

AARON BETSKY

Designed by Andrew Bromberg of Aedas, The Star is a remarkable building that does double duty as a performance venue hoisted above a shopping mall. Yet beyond its role as an object building, it also explores the notion of what constitutes contemporary civic or public space and the changing forces that anchor and give meaning to the urban scene.

Historically, public space and civic monuments are the building blocks of the city. In particular, public space is regarded as being somehow free and noble. It should not belong to anybody, unless it is the state or community. It should be able to accommodate different uses and mediate between the interests of different groups to maintain a harmonious civic balance. In its most ideal form, it should both make room for and give expression to a shared vision of the community or state. It should be a place of and for democracy.

Yet it is difficult to identify places that fulfil such criteria, beyond the momentary conversion of Cairo's Tahrir Square or the Washington Mall into sites of popular protest. And public space as defined today is a relatively recent phenomenon. Before the mid 19th century it was not easy to find spaces that were consciously designed for public use, apart from market squares at the heart of the city and commons outside it. The former were primarily places of commerce but not always in use, so other activities could take place, while the latter were sites for agriculture. Other 'public' spaces included roads, which were essentially sites of transit, and parade grounds where ruling regimes displayed their power. The closest most Western cities came to public space was the area in front of a church or cathedral. Generally this was reserved for outside rituals and the gathering of the faithful as they filed in or out, but it could also host different kinds of uses.

With the development of squares, *allées* and parks, the middle class invented public space. Here, the bourgeoisie could show off during their leisure time, or gather to flaunt their newly acquired power and social importance. In these new public arenas they could preen and define themselves, reinforcing values of order, clarity, openness and a relative lack of hierarchy. Middle-class public space connected to civic monuments – such as town halls, parliaments, law courts, opera houses and museums – has effectively shaped the modern city, leaving the once potent emblems of aristocratic or ecclesiastic rule as isolated remnants within its ever-spreading grid.

Now, however, the character of modern public space is more difficult to define. Except in Mediterranean countries, the idea of promenading or simply wandering around has disappeared. Democracy takes place through new online communities or in strictly controlled gatherings. Open space is increasingly precious and under pressure. In many cities, it is the domain of *flâneurs* and tourists, admiring the relics of lost epochs. As it disappears, the cries for its preservation intensify, without a clear sense of how it could be reused, a dilemma compounded by changing social, economic and technological factors.

'All conditioned space is conditional,' wrote Rem Koolhaas, and of course, there are limits to how commercialised public space is used and who can use it. Today, perhaps the 'freest' kind of public space is the internet, where social media provide ways to create connections, arrive at collective opinions, or just hang out. Despite recent revelations making it clear that the scrutiny of this virtual domain is more intense than originally thought, digital networks still remain highly effective at creating instant communities.

4. (Right) like a
giant architectural
millefeuille, layering
and fragmentation
give **The Star's** facades
a hectic dynamism

masterplan of One North development

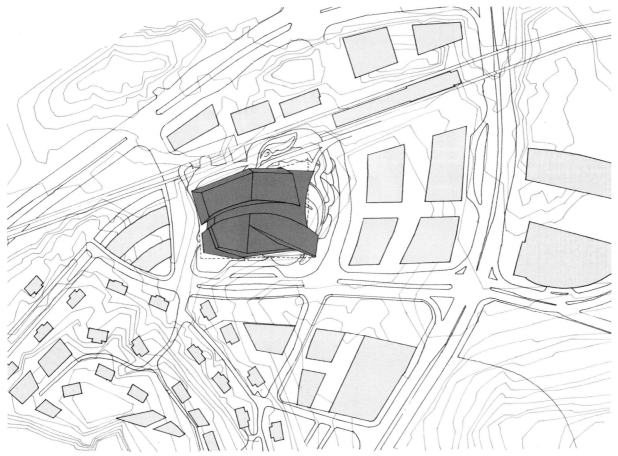

site plan

What remains of physical public space tends to exist on the fringes, often hosting semi-illegal activities and gatherings, from raves to sexual couplings. Shopping malls are a more mainstream form of public encounter, where people promenade, exercise, meet each other and engender a sense of community, however tenuous. Transport hubs such as airports and train stations are another kind of modern public space, but also tend to be structured around retail activity.

Apart from shopping, the other key catalyst for public space is spectacle. We live in a society of spectacle, as culture and sport increasingly embrace the spectacular. Even religion has assumed this dimension, as traditional places of worship give way to mega churches whose rites channel the spectacle of staged entertainment and whose reach extends out infinitely through electronic media.

Good public space provides a lacuna, a break, a sense of nothing. It is the void that stands against the increasingly dense matrix of the urban core. Outside this centre, in the domain of sprawl, its defined character offers a visible and experiential version of the miasmic spaces around it. It also is a place to do nothing, not to work, not to play a role, and not to engage in economic relations with anybody. True public space is a place to be. Yet in socio-economic terms, this functionlessness is increasingly difficult to justify. After all, doing nothing is generally considered odd or unacceptable.

As contemporary public space migrates into places of commerce, and the anchors that give meaning to the urban realm are no longer the containers of public space, but places of spectacle, the success of The Star can be easily understood. Acting as a powerful new landmark in a suburban part of Singapore, it combines commercialised public space with a place of spectacle.

5. The Star anchors the still-evolving area, conveying a strong sense of spectacle, but also a sense of generous and inhabitable public space
6. Hoisted on angular pilotis, the auditorium shelters the shopping and socialising area below

diagram showing functional relationships

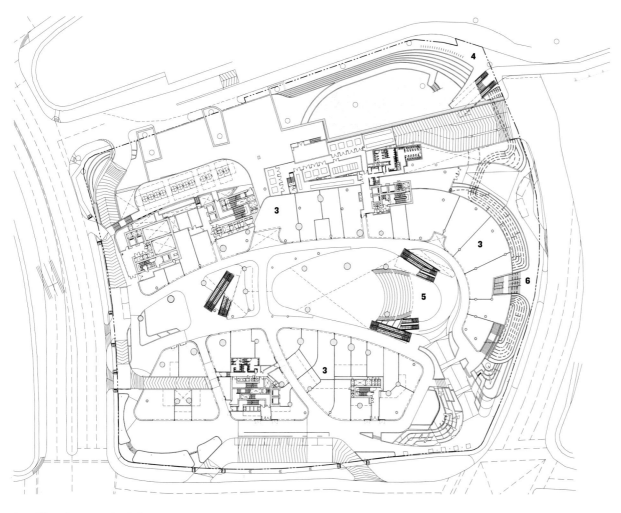

ground floor plan: open-air retail

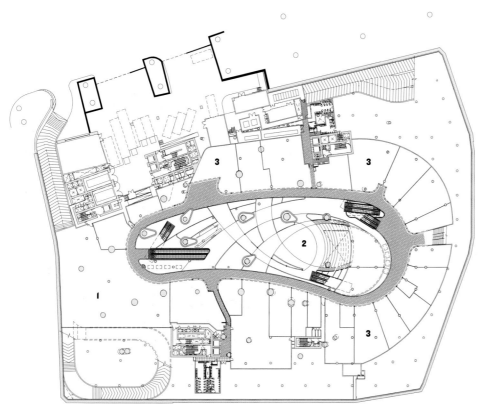

basement plan: retail piazza

1 gourmet supermarket
2 civic piazza
3 shop units
4 connection to MRT station
5 retail amphitheatre
6 entrance to retail piazza
7 food court
8 restaurants
9 function halls
10 studios
11 theatre lobby
12 trap room beneath stage
13 skylight
14 stage
15 5,000 seat theatre
16 roof terrace
17 VIP rooms

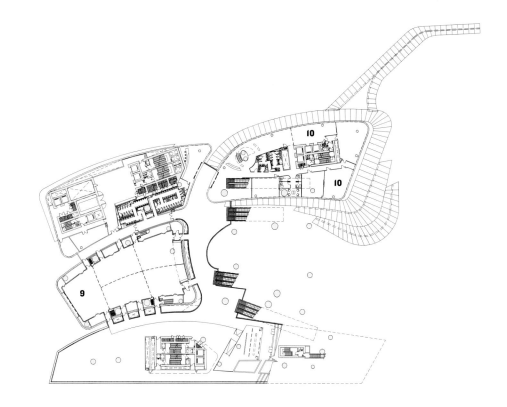

second floor plan: civic level

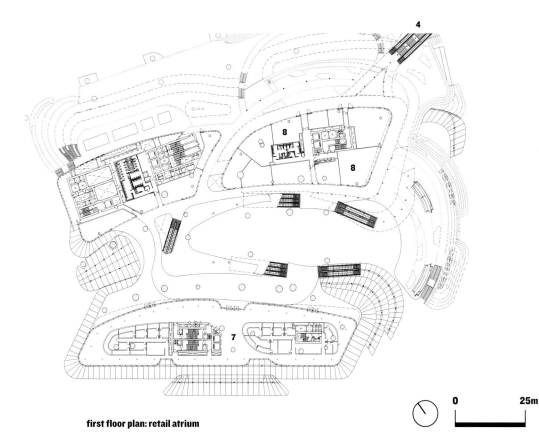

'The building's open
appearance and fragmented
monumentality make
it a place that effortlessly
absorbs people and events'

first floor plan: retail atrium

0   25m

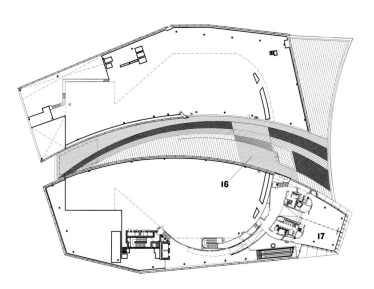

tenth floor plan: upper function hall

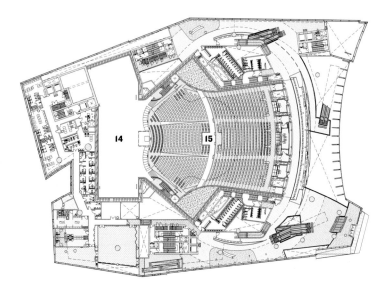

eighth floor plan: auditorium

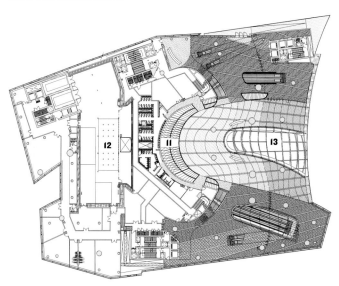

fourth floor plan: theatre atrium

7. (Previous page)
glazed canopies fan
out from the base
of the building, offering
protection from
the elements.
Singapore's hot, humid
climate encourages
outdoor living and
The Star is designed to
take advantage of this
8 (Opposite) & 9.
A mixture of opaque and
translucent cladding
animates the building's
sculptural profile
10. Detail of external
cladding panels

'Seen from the elevated train
track, The Star insistently
looms and swells over the
station, making it the most
obvious place to head on arrival'

Asian cities do not generally have the same tradition of European or American public space, although many developed along those lines as they became more exposed to Western influences. Asian public space is more intensely commercialised, with fewer qualms about its open status. Parks and open spaces have specific uses, and their design usually does not promote or encourage unstructured gathering. 'Spontaneous' public spaces often arise by happenstance, at the fringe, or for a particular reason. The lively and unexpected colonisation of the covered base of the HSBC headquarters in Hong Kong as an informal meeting place for off-duty maids is perhaps the most famous example.

In Singapore, the combination of a desire to create a multi-ethnic national identity and to research into urban planning, from which bureaucrats apprehended that lively public spaces are a prerequisite of attractive cities, has resulted in a concerted effort to create and promote public space. For a city-state seeking actively to compete for inhabitants and investment, this is now seen as an essential aspect of how it functions and how it is judged.

Lying north-west of Singapore's Downtown Core, One North was originally developed in 2001 to a masterplan by Zaha Hadid. Despite Hadid's strongly defined layout, the development remains a bland and slightly desolate array of office buildings. Although its public spaces are landscaped with care and impeccably maintained, the monofunctional character of the area and hot, humid climate result in the public realm not being well-used, adding to a sense of surburban anomie.

Located next to a mass transit stop, The Star provides an alternative. Shaded yet open, it is a highly visible magnet for people and activities. Programmatically, its many restaurants, cafés and bars (which account for over half the units) attract people at almost all times of day, while events bring in crowds during the weekends and evenings. The building's open appearance and fragmented monumentality make it a place that effortlessly absorbs people and events. Its auditorium presents itself as a structure that is so different, so complex, and so miraculously heavy as it hovers benignly over the shopping spaces below.

Bromberg's design of The Star transforms it into a place of spectacle and modern public space. Most obvious of these is the complexity of the building's shape and the manner in which materials give expression to the forms. Confronting the vacant lot in front of it (soon to be filled by another structure), The Star presents a boldly bifurcated prow. Each half consists of plates that slide and rotate away from each other, reinforcing the building's mass by catching your eye, yet also breaking down its monumental scale into different elements wrapped in a silvery skin. Seen from the elevated train track, The Star insistently looms and swells over the station, making it the most obvious place to head for on arrival.

A concave glass curve recedes invitingly, while the base of the building oozes out into a tongue-shaped protuberance. Against this, the land berms up, curving around from the direction of the station and propelling you to the main entrance. Glass canopies fan out in greeting and the pavement slopes down as it lures you into the building's heart.

Here, the spatial drama really begins. Broad, curving stairs splay out and lead you down into its depths (an escalator offers a shortcut). Muscular columns incline forward, as if straining to hold up the mass of the auditorium above. Stores and restaurants encircle you, opening up to a piazza on the level below. The concave glass of the facade continues into this open atrium, swinging up to allow glimpses of the performance area's lobby.

AR | AEDAS **25**

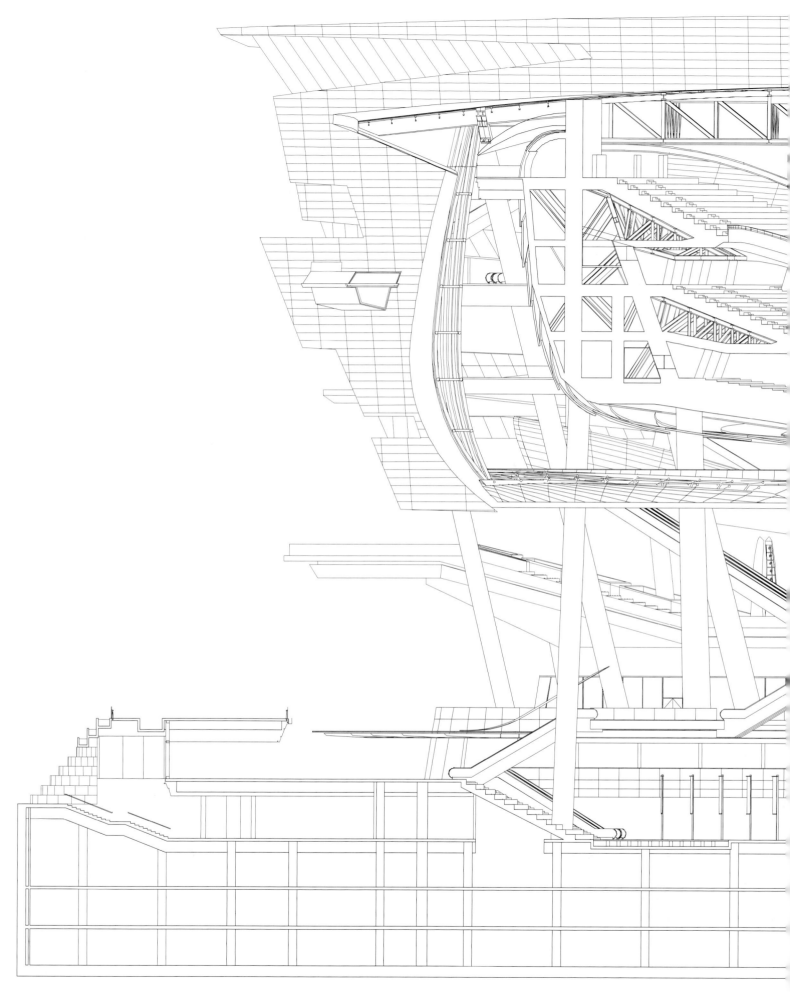

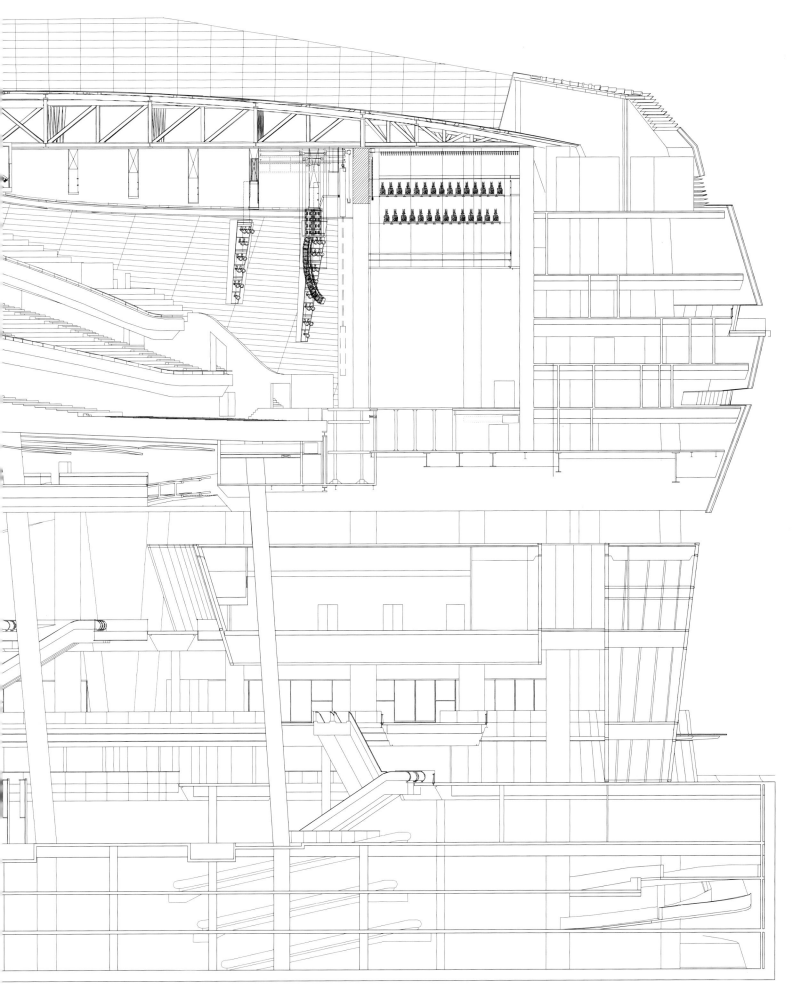

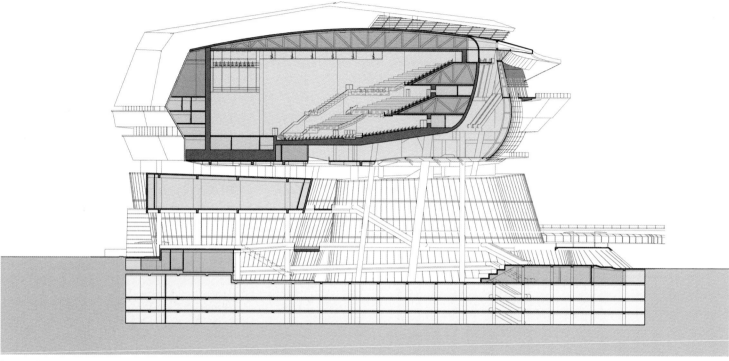

long section

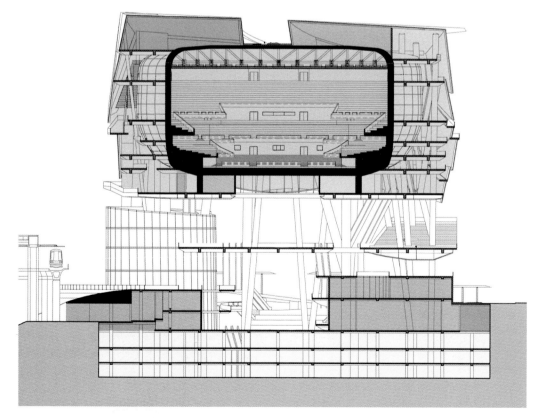

cross section

The spatial fluidity continues into the retail corridors that extend back from this central space leading to more restaurants deployed around the building's side and rear.

What is most remarkable about this space is that it is open to the outdoors. Bromberg has kept environmental conditioning to the absolute minimum, confining it to the stores and restaurants. Rejecting the default template of the air-conditioned mall, it attempts to create experiential continuity between indoors and outdoors. There are, for instance, many open-air stalls. This concept is not new in Singapore, where the warm climate and cooling breezes mean that such spaces can be used almost continuously, as long as they are sheltered from the effects of rain and sun.

Everything flows, with a minimum of barriers. As a result, The Star's base is a genuinely modern public space. Sheltered from the harsher aspects of the elements, filled with places to sit, watch and be watched (including a small outdoor amphitheatre on an upper level), it slows the motion of daily life through its streams and eddies of space, creating a sense not so much of separate, self-enclosed realm, as a version of the outdoor neighbourhood that invites communal activities or observation. Yet this is not to say that The Star is not dedicated to selling things, and that the kind of community it creates is not conditioned. The character it conveys and expects of its inhabitants is that of a certain clean-cut excitement: painted white, collaging rather clashing, its forms are in the domain of the benevolent whale-like volume that floats above it.

This volume, which generated the building in the first place, is a 5,000-seat auditorium built by the commercial arm of the New Creation Church (called Rock Productions), which uses it for its weekend services. The Church's offices surmount the shopping mall,

developed by CapitaMalls in collaboration with Rock Productions, and, as you rise on long escalators through the forest of abstracted columns, you find yourself in a more tranquil enclave. Bromberg made it a point to continue the unconditioned, outdoor space as far as possible, even using exiting requirements to create a path that would allow you to travel all the way to the building's roof and back down without entering either conditioned or ticketed spaces.

Ultimately, however, you do enter into the realm of air conditioning and control. Yet Bromberg has also ensured that there is at least a visual connection to the public realm as you survey the atrium below and the surroundings through what from the inside resembles a billowing sail. Forms subside into waves of white plaster, the lobby's roof lowers, and all lines lead to the auditorium.

Inside, the spectacle of the auditorium unfolds in an explosive and all-consuming swoop. The floor arches out to fill almost the whole width of the building, while a wide stage opens up to meet the rows of spectators. Low-slung balconies push forward from the recesses. Here, the Star's architecture, which from the outside appears so multitudinous, so cacophonous, so layered and so assertive, finally defers to its core purpose: to provide distraction in the form of rituals, faith or an ecstatic escapism that temporarily takes you out of the real world. For the auditorium, Bromberg creates a compact container for spectacle that does its job without overwhelming the performances that take place in it.

Ironically, the building's black box heart, and the reason for its construction in the first place, is perhaps the least interesting part of the structure. It is well designed, but does not catch the eye or give anything back to its function. Yet crucially, rather than being

12. (Previous spread) cooled by air currents that flow through the soaring volume, The Star's shopping atrium reconceives the notion of public space for the modern tropical city
13, 14. At night the foyer spaces around the auditorium come alive with concert-goers
15. (Opposite) banks of escalators wind up to the auditorium, offering vertiginous views en route

'Rejecting the default template of the air-conditioned mall, it attempts to create experiential continuity between indoors and outdoors'

16. (Opposite) the lobby and spaces around the auditorium form a setting for social interaction, as a place to see and be seen 17. At the heart of the building is a 5,000 seat auditorium, a container for performance spectacle 18. (Overleaf) in the context of The Star's frenetic architectural language, the auditorium is a calmer enclave, yet it has a sense of drama and grandeur nonetheless

embedded below ground, passively entombed, the auditorium is actively used to attract, shelter and stage many different sorts of communal activities. Bromberg combines the notion of icon and public space to create a container for urban spectacle.

In skilfully easing public space out of a shopping mall, Bromberg encourages all manner of uses and patterns of circulation. The Star's base opens and entices; the shops curve into a hospitable and welcoming arena. It is still an unashamedly commercial armature, but one in which the containers and sellers of goods or food are only one aspect of a space that seeks to reclaim the elusive sense of not doing anything. You can simply sit and watch the world go by.

Though The Star has a geological solidity, like a massive fractured rock face, Bromberg hints rather than shows, alludes rather than points, and intimates rather than imitates, transforming the vast structure into an enigma and attractor. The Star thus takes its place in a global repertoire of consciously conspicuous civic buildings, whose lineage extends all the way from Sydney's Opera House, via the Bilbao Guggenheim to the Dalian Conference Center, Guangzhou Opera House and Hamburg Philharmonic. Each has replaced the more traditional didactic exemplars of middle-class power with stranger, more amorphous structures, designed for shifting communities that are equally difficult to define.

So it is with The Star and the way it unites churchgoers and shoppers, office workers and commuters, bringing them together around something that none can identify, but all can identify with. And in its hybrid nature and complex architecture, it also provides a model for how expressive form-making deployed in the service of place can redefine the notion of habitable, engaged, public space in the modern tropical city.

STRUCTURAL FORCES

On a cramped site, with an unconventional arrangement of an auditorium sitting above a shopping centre, The Star's structural design is necessarily efficient and inventive, says *Matthew Wells*

The Star's structure achieves its over-scaled effect by a fluent deployment of conventional means. Reinforced-concrete parking basements form the foundation to a sunken piazza and tiered shopping mall. High-strength concrete columns and vertical circulation cores then extend upwards to support composite steel and concrete floors framed with fabricated steel sections and truss elements. High occupancy levels on the upper levels punch out large core areas and these provide lateral bracing to the slender raking columns.

The sectional arrangement of a large auditorium over a public space, defining and sheltering it, has precedents extending back to the revolving halls of Vladimir Tatlin's Monument to the Third International. Examples by Massimiliano Fuksas and Richard Rogers for the Rome Congress Centre rely on a head-frame to suspend their theatre-volumes, demarcating the public space below and giving their enclosures sculptural presence.

In reaching the tipping point of practicality, The Star is structured like a layer cake, an extrapolation of a podium building where the transfer structure is broadened into a deck sufficient to carry a tiered auditorium, foyers and ancillary spaces. The critical nuance is in limiting the perimeter screens to create a microclimate around an open-air shopping mall, with the central piazza conceived as a pool of cool air. Shade, shelter and natural breeze (not stack effects) are manipulated to overstep the limitation of air-conditioned arcades and atria towards a new retail and leisure experience for the tropics.

The structural design of The Star relies on the analysis systems, materials innovation and contractor capabilities currently available, but it is an imaginative use of such tools. It employs four-dimensional analysis programmes (three axes of strain and one of time) to ensure that large spans can be created with manageable building movements during construction and minimal vibration in the auditorium areas. It is also a means not only of managing complex form, assessing its cost and making manufacture practical and economic, but also of achieving an interlocking of systems in one form. The building is studied in many ways: as a free-form structure, as a circulation system without bottlenecks, as light modulator and wind sculpture. Computational fluid dynamics (CFD) and heat flow modelling allow the interactions of form and environment to be predicted and modified. This is about tapping into the nature of things – not just materials but also circulation systems, air and heat flows and, of course, light.

The creation of computer models is time-consuming and expensive. They tend to channel the design process. The Star was fixed in a sketch from day one, so relatively full models were developed and added to. Findings on air flows and rain penetration prompted local adjustments, additions of canopies and landscape components.

1. (Previous page) an irregular grid of inclined columns rises from the basement to support the atrium and auditorium
2. (Final spread) the building under construction showing the integration of the main structural elements

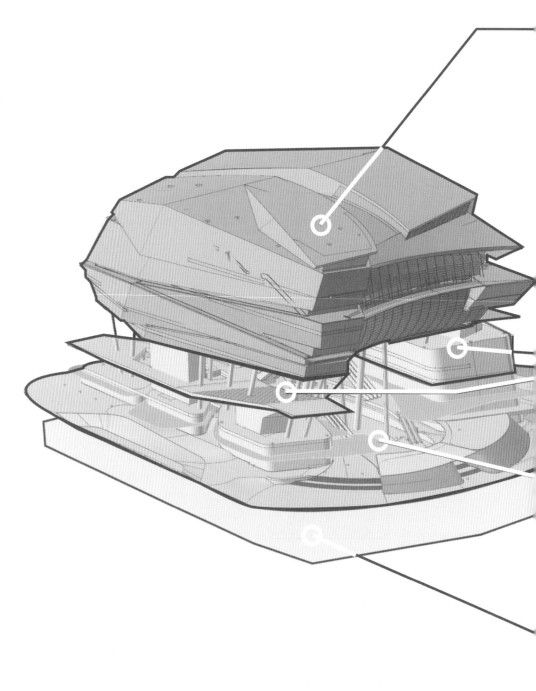

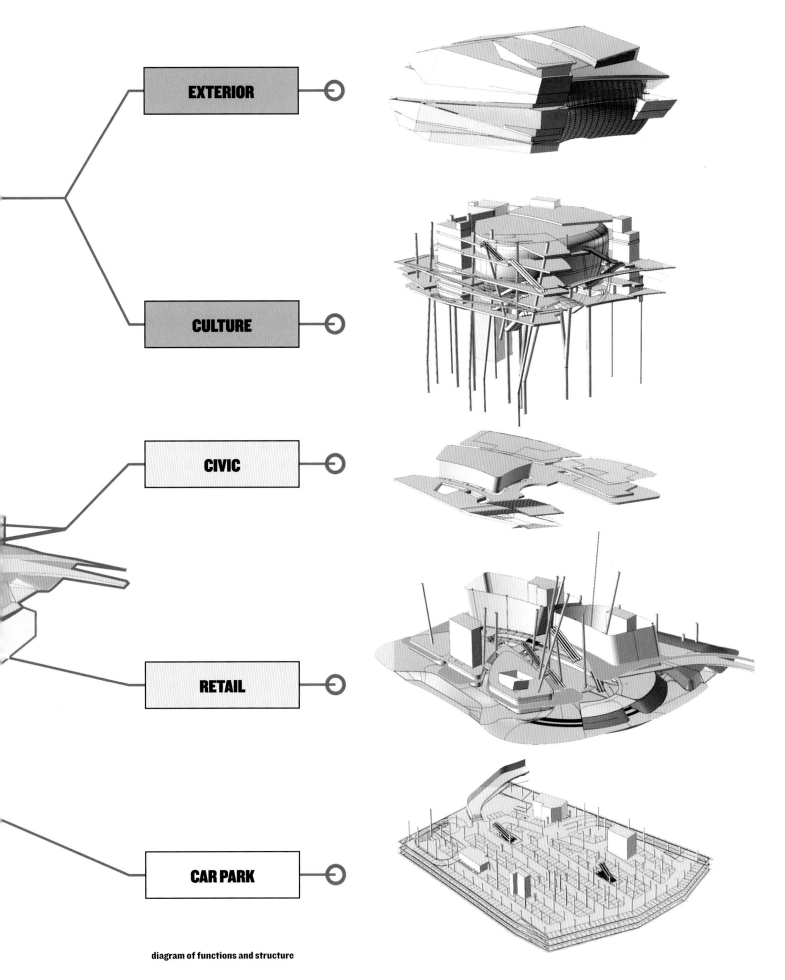

EXTERIOR

CULTURE

CIVIC

RETAIL

CAR PARK

diagram of functions and structure

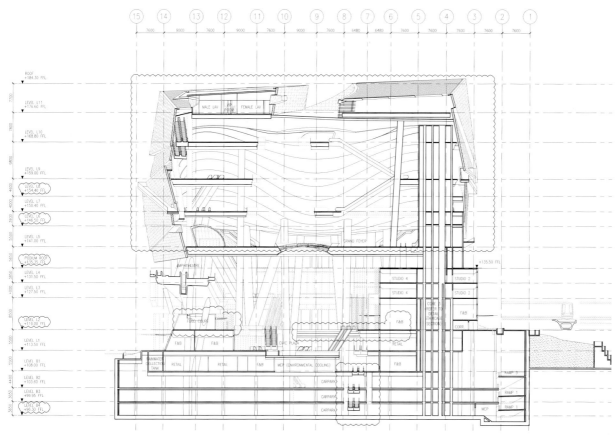

setting out drawing through the atrium

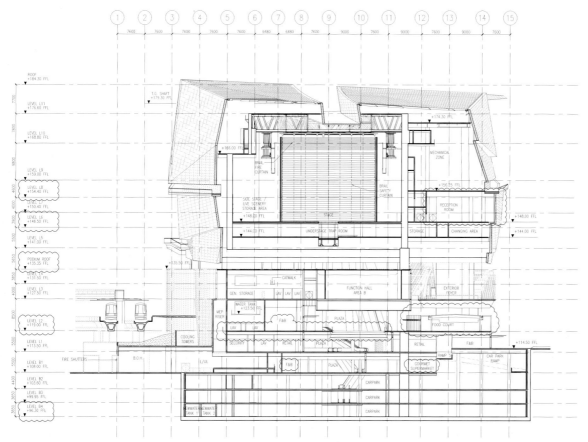

setting out drawing through the auditorium

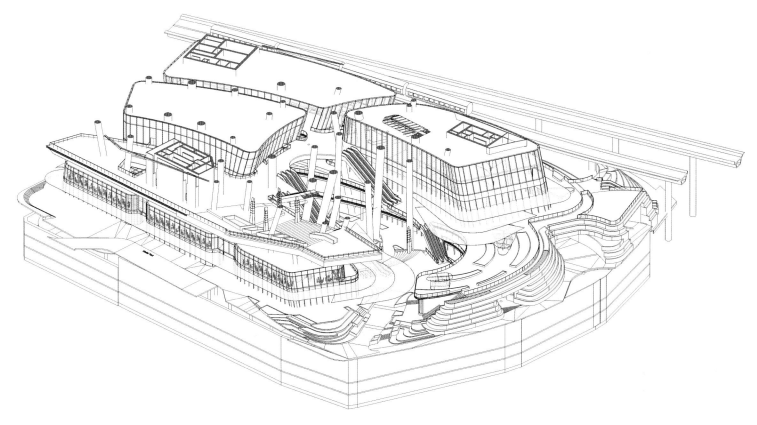

podium showing structure and service cores

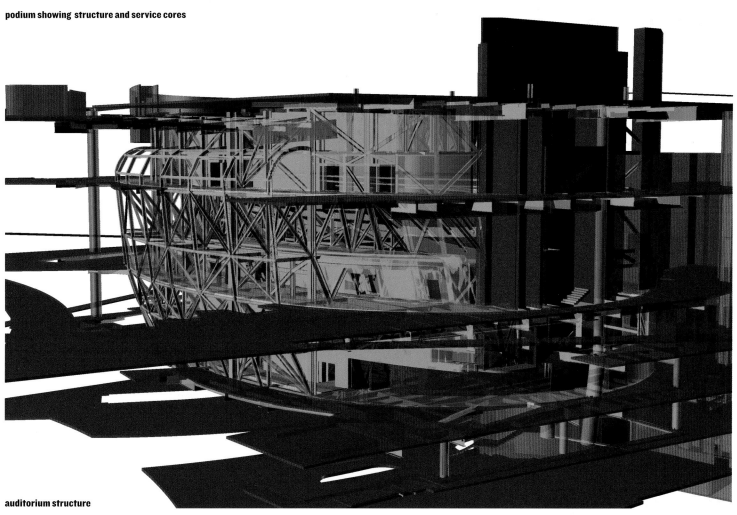

auditorium structure

If a project of this complexity is the outcome of an orchestrated variety of inputs, rather like a film production crew rallying to the will of an auteur, then it's fair to judge contributions in their own terms. For instance, the second-unit work on structure, the suspended front screen and the large borrowed-light and smoke screen grid shell over the public space are exemplary understated lightweight screens, delicate set pieces. In the process of this compartmentalisation junctions shade out and details absent themselves.

The reliance on a napkin sketch seems curiously steampunk in this computer age. It circumvents the contemporary tendency to create built diagrams, but perhaps the very complexity of a building like this one will overcome that issue in a different way.

The question going forward is whether the deployment of these computer systems will break across the individual architect's vision, creating in themselves an architecture or just a pile of stuff. In this respect, structure is no longer about setting a default position, the grid, but enabling access to something more.

As early as 1978 in an article on Alvar Aalto, Demetri Porphyrios recognised a coming design sensibility of 'heterotopic ordering'. This is not just giving each influence equal status but allowing each incommensurable its ideal form. Architects choose their own preoccupations. Hans Scharoun's buildings work around circulation and light, occasionally acoustics, with air flows irrelevant. Richard Meier used to dissect out structure, circulation and enclosure and then effect a recombination of volumes in light. Frank Gehry's models sit at the centre of his studio as elements of pure form, added to and subtracted. Now all these strategies can have a machine-made component. The architect is presented with a mixing desk.

The Star is a unique building and a precedent that others will follow. As the typology develops, the engineering of environment in particular will be felt. Simpler, elemental models more amenable to change and development will guide the designer's hand. The process will follow through a hierarchy of models, successive elaborations. Jan Kaplicky worked up several schemes in which wind-tunnel studies and CFDs generated form as well as justifying it. Parametricism establishes overt linkages between the dimensions of a problem. The designer chooses the quotients that will govern.

The success of The Star should be judged in terms of – what? Air flows, of course; anyone who has experienced Singapore will know that. Raffles is perfectly proportioned. One final thing in this profusion of additions. Having worked up such architectural complexity, it's often necessary to strip it back to essentials. Think Coco Chanel. Before leaving the house look in the mirror and remove one accessory. Yet buildings of this richness may not need that discipline.

CLIMATE CONTROL

The Star's strategy for environmental control exploits and optimises natural sources of cooling, says *Henry Luker*

I. (Previous page)
though individual shop
units are air conditioned,
the main volume
of the shopping centre
is naturally cooled
2. The open undercroft
captures cooling breezes
3. Mechanical fans assist
with air circulation

Comfort and delight are good ambitions for any building, particularly public spaces that need to attract people to be viable. The same is true when thinking about good environmental design: sustainability and energy conservation, though important, must not come at the expense of comfort. A perfectly sustainable building that is unpleasant to occupy is not really sustainable at all.

Comfort can be a difficult subject. It is subjective and is much more than just thermal comfort. It is a feeling about the whole space, which also involves context, culture and expectation. Within the context of passive design, architects often need to explore the limits of what's acceptable to those who will use the building. The starting point is the local climate.

Singapore is not particularly hot in comparison to global extremes – the annual average air temperature ranges between 24 deg C and 32 deg C. However, it does have very high humidity, averaging around 84 per cent. It is this, and the intense sun if you cannot find shade, that has the greatest impact. The region's architecture has developed in response to this climate and the human desire to find comfort. If you consider a traditional home in this part of the world, it is built with a large overhanging roof to provide shade from the sun and shelter from the frequent rainstorms. It also features open sides to maximise the cooling effects of prevailing winds. When coupled with adequate shade, this air movement is the critical factor in providing comfort. Yet its importance is often overlooked within modern sealed, air-conditioned environments.

Aedas's design response has embraced the local context, and the practice has drawn extensively on its knowledge of traditional design techniques to manage the tropical climate. This makes The Star a very modern and not immediately obvious interpretation of this vernacular. The concert hall, which needs to be sealed and conditioned by necessity, plays an important role. By being raised and left exposed, it provides the crucial

podium landscaping plan

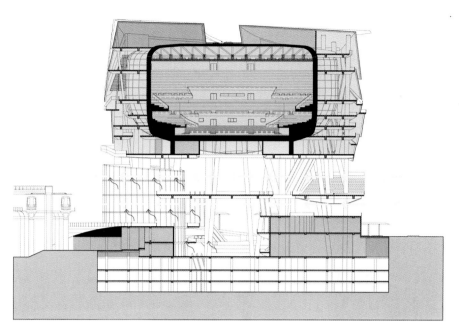

cross section showing airflow patterns

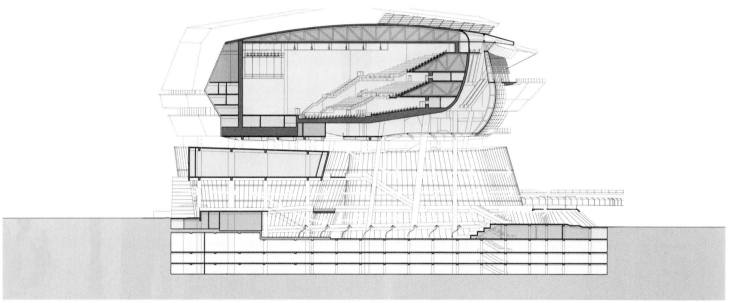

long section showing airflow patterns

2

3

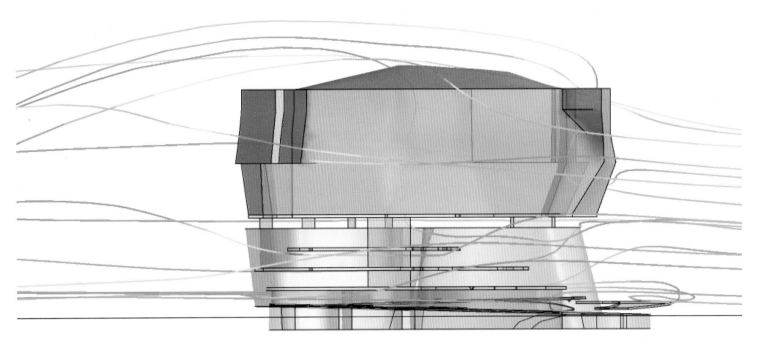

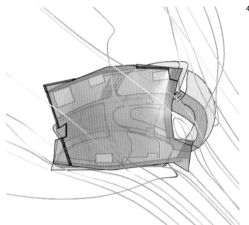

airflow modelling work

shade and weather protection to the open shopping centre below. Openings into the centre are positioned to collect the prevailing breezes, with the building form around the openings carefully shaped to capture it and increase its intensity. The use of mechanical fans to supplement this natural breeze on very still or exceptionally warm days is a sensible and necessary precaution. The shops, which are air conditioned, provide benefits as well. Cool air leaking out through the entrances is of obvious assistance. But it is the low radiant temperature (another important factor in comfort) of the glazed shop fronts that is probably of more significance.

The way in which Bromberg designed and managed the openings into the shopping mall plays an important role, more psychological than physiological. If you have to walk through a physical barrier to enter an enclosed space your expectations are very different. And if the conditions for an enclosed space matched the open spaces of The Star then many would deem them unacceptable. So the way we perceive a space is important to our feelings of wellbeing. But by making the shopping mall an extension of the outside – part of the journey to the shops – Aedas has exploited this psychological effect to the full.

The Star is an impressive example of holistic design that works with the local climate rather than fighting against it. The design team has clearly demonstrated their understanding of the many factors involved in making people comfortable and has responded to this in a way that minimises the need for energy-intensive interventions. Yet having good ideas is only one aspect of the equation. Perhaps even more important was the way the design team was prepared to challenge preconceptions of what a shopping mall should be. Equally important in this equation was a client willing to listen to new ideas with an open mind. But the most convincing endorsement comes from the people who use it. It has clearly been embraced and the people of Singapore have decisively made it their own.

4. The transition from exterior to interior is seamless. Unlike more conventional air-conditioned malls, The Star is a genuinely inside/outside space
5. Open landscaped decks encircle the building allowing air to circulate around the interior

BUILDING THE STAR

The scale and complexity of The Star's construction, achieved in just forty months, is captured in this series of site shots

5

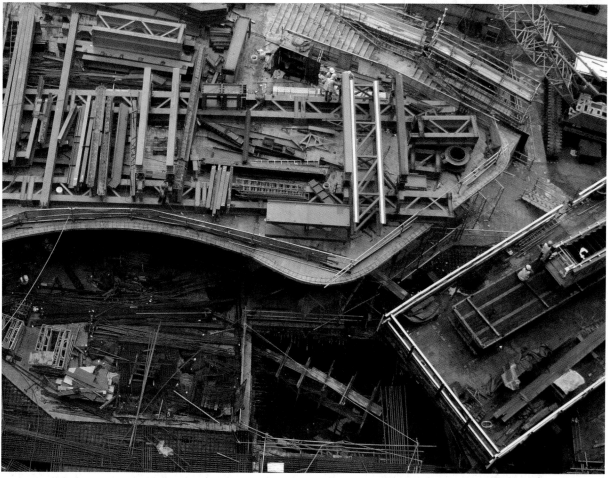

6

1. (Opening spread, left) a delicate lattice of scaffolding rises through the huge shopping atrium
2. (Opening spread, right) the form of the building is slowly becoming visible
3. (Previous spread, top) angular columns support the auditorium
4. (Previous spread, bottom) the steel-framed structure of the auditorium takes shape
5. Detail of the steel trusses supporting the billowing glass wall
6. Aerial view of the site showing the curved form of the atrium floors
7. (Opposite) sunlight rakes the angular columns of the atrium in an almost Piranesian tableau
8. (Overleaf) scaffolding fills the auditorium

A DAY IN THE LIFE

As an accommodating armature for culture, shopping and socialising, The Star reconceptualises notions of public urban space in the tropics

1. (Previous page, left) sheltered by the volume of the auditorium, the shopping centre is an animated and enticing public space that is constantly in use
2. (Previous page, right) lush greenery gives the open spaces an informal, park-like feel
3. (Opposite) The Star is the antithesis of the sealed, air-conditioned mall. Glass canopies offer protection against the intense tropical rain
4. Public furniture is robust yet sculptural
5. Eating alfresco at one of the many restaurants
6. Browsing in an open-air book market
7. Ramps connect The Star with the street, channelling people into its many attractions
8. Children playing in the central fountain

'Light, air and greenery penetrate the heart of the building, creating a sense of sybaritic, tropical luxuriance'

'The Star is brought to life by a constant stream of people shopping, eating, meeting friends or attending events in the auditorium'

9. Visitors watching the world go by from one of the walkways
10. Sunday morning church service in the auditorium. The enthusiastic congregation of the New Creation Church fills the 5,000 seat hall
11, 12. Shopping and socialising in the mall
13. The central fountain can be transformed into a space for relaxing and watching performances
14. (Opposite) the tiered open-air theatre attracts a crowd

'After dark, the vast auditorium and its network of foyer spaces comes alive with all kinds of concert-goers'

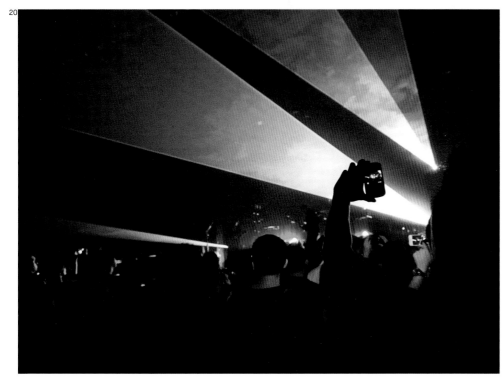

15. (Opposite) ramps and walkways threaded around the perimeter of the building offer views of the surroundings
16. *Brief Encounter* Singapore style on one of the escalators
17. After dark, mingling in the dramatic foyer spaces
18. Setting up for a concert in the auditorium
19. Oliver Sim of British indie pop band The xx performing on stage at The Star in early August
20. A rapt audience shows its appreciation

CITY STATE

Recent architecture in Singapore has tended
to ignore its tropical context, but The Star
provides a possible paradigm for a new form of
sustainable design, says *Patrick Bingham-Hall*

So much has been built in 21st-century Singapore – a city unscathed by even a hint of an economic crisis since 1997 – but so much of the architecture has been inappropriate in its context and misguided in its aspiration. No matter how persuasively a client's desire for a transparently ephemeral style is phrased, no architect designing in a tropical city should ever forsake the greater obligation to ensure sustainable and climatically attuned construction. And, it would be nice to think that no architect would ever shun the opportunity to respond respectfully and expressively to the genius loci. Yet forsake and shun they have, in droves. Much of the public and commercial architecture has made little or no concession to the tropical context, too many of the buildings have been cold-climate models that could have been built anywhere in the

world, and as rumours would have it, some of them were in fact designed for cities that have a winter and then expediently transported to a new equatorial home without modification.

The aesthetic and structural incongruity of contemporary tropical architecture is, of course, easily explained. A preference for air conditioning has (for all manner of reasons) become a prerequisite, and air-conditioned volumes need to be enclosed. The best that most architects can do is play around the edges and devise a fringe of tropicality, which signals a quasi engagement rather than a fundamental response. Truly tropical architecture in Asia (as categorised in formal histories) prefigured air conditioning: either in the form of vernacular structures with regional variations, or as heroic 20th-century Modernist interventions in a Third World setting.

Singapore missed out in both ways: its vernacular architecture was colonial rather than indigenous, and Modernism did not have enough time to indulge in climatic innovation before the advent of air conditioning, which was infamously referred to by Lee Kuan Yew as the greatest invention of the 20th century. During the city's pragmatic and rapidly accelerating growth following independence in 1965, few local architects, or the ubiquitous imported A-listers, proposed an alternative to the hermetic sealing of large-scale projects. However, as irony inevitably pursues reality, Singapore's ascendance in Southeast Asia was effectively symbolised in the eyes of its not-yet-emerging neighbours by swathes of scrupulously modern public housing estates that relied upon passive, vernacular-derived, low-cost environmental strategies to provide

ventilation and livability. Then, in the 1980s, as the unprecedented evidence of global warming begat the glimmer of a notion of sustainable architecture, an approach now categorised as 'tropical Modernism' was proffered as a possibility, although the intimidating implications of derailing the generic aesthetics of Singapore's corporate image-building meant that any propositions were largely conceptual, and initially implemented at a small scale.

Tay Kheng Soon was the proselytiser in chief in the '80s, pointing out the elephant in the room: an absurd acquiescence to an architecture that prescribed a potentially ruinous over-reliance upon air conditioning. Practising as Akitek Tenggara, one of Tay's earliest projects – Parkway Builders' Centre (1985) – comprised 13 floors of offices on an L plan, which looked over a naturally ventilated

atrium clad with two walls of glass louvres. Although formally unadventurous, the scheme unambiguously resolved a fundamental problem that lingers, larger than ever, in 2013: the stupendously wasteful use of energy required to air-condition massive volumes in public buildings. Airports, office complexes, shopping malls and hotels throughout tropical Asia feature monumentally redundant spaces – atria, lobbies, pedestrian links – that could either be radically reduced in size or naturally shaded and ventilated. Possibly Tay's most notable achievement was the Kandang Kerbau Hospital (completed in 1997), graphically depicting its programme of passive solar protection in a manner that drew comparisons with the buildings of Ken Yeang in Malaysia. Yeang had long advocated climate-responsive architecture, and he was to design two

buildings in Singapore – the National Library (AR July 2005) and Solaris (2010) – that were clinical implementations of his 'bioclimatic' strategies, which incorporated solar buffers, wind-scoops, double layers of sun screens, sky gardens and open-to-the-elements atria.

Despite the prolific perpetuation of inappropriate architecture by architects who should know better, Singapore's 21st-century architecture has been tangibly defined by a series of projects that respond unequivocally to the delights of the tropics, and which make a virtue of their climate-control devices. Will Alsop, for example, positively revelled in the transformation of Clarke Quay (2006), where two pedestrianised streets of restored shophouses were sheltered by massive transparent 'umbrellas' and cooled by breezes from large low-speed fans with lotus-root faces.

1. (Previous pages) Singapore's skyline is rapidly evolving around the central business core
2. With a limited island land mass, the cultivation of high density, for both commercial and residential developments, is seen as essential to Singapore's ability to accommodate its growing population. Here the new towers of the central commercial district loom over Chinatown, characterised by the traditional two-storey live/work shophouses which historically made up Singapore's urban grain
3. Marina Bay Sands Hotel by Moshe Safdie in association with Aedas was developed by the Sands gambling consortium. The model is the Las Vegas casino hotel, spectacularly recast for Singapore
4. Container ships waiting to dock in Singapore's cargo port. In terms of tonnage, the port is the world's second busiest
5. Reflections at Keppel Bay by Daniel Libeskind, a development of housing towers and villas on Singapore's historic harbour
6. Detail of one of Singapore's many exuberant Hindu temples

'Much public and commercial architecture has made little or no concession to the tropical climate'

8

'The Star can be seen as a contemporary prototype for genuinely sustainable architecture'

The Khoo Teck Puat Hospital (2010, designed by RMJM Hillier with CPG Consultants) calibrated massing, orientation, breezeways as tunnels, layers of planting, groves of trees and a multitude of screening devices, to create a spectacular (and literally) green building-as-landscape. Over a broad range of typologies, WOHA has produced a canon of work with a varied and occasionally audacious appearance, and in preparation for a non-air-conditioned future, the practice has been pushing at the boundaries of structural permutation. Externally draped with a cloak of green vines, the School of the Arts (AR June 2011) is WOHA's most uncompromising Singapore structure: an 11-storey space-frame containing massive voids, separated by galleries of one-room-thick classrooms and continuously linked by open-ended breezeways.

Structural microenvironments – emphatic manipulations of ground planes, elements and spaces – may eventually constitute the only viable minimum-energy form of construction in 21st-century tropical Asia. The Star can thus be seen as a contemporary prototype for genuinely sustainable architecture, and as part of a constantly evolving elaboration of the 'tropical Modernism' of a previous generation. The articulation of the two most fundamental principles of tropical passive design – natural ventilation and shading – is so exaggerated and so uninhibited that the architecture also signals a reprise of the heroic ideals of Modernist structural expression, when architects had no desire to obscure their functional and programmatic intentions, and little inclination to conform to prevailing orthodoxy.

FOUR FOR THE FUTURE

From a new rail terminus in Hong Kong to an unbuilt dance centre in the Netherlands, this quartet of projects shows the diversity of Andrew Bromberg's work in concept and practice

1. The newly completed CX 2-1 in Singapore forms part of the same One North development as The Star
2. Exhibition centre in Guangzhou embraces dramatic scale and form
3. Still under construction, the Express Rail Link West Kowloon Terminus will be a new rail gateway to Hong Kong
4. Model of a competition proposal for a new dance centre in The Hague

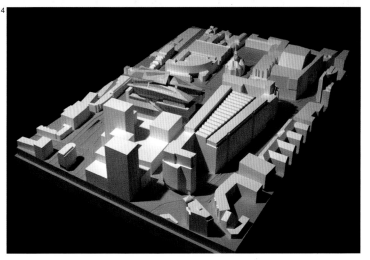

CIVIC OFFICE

A new regional headquarters for one of the world's leading entertainment companies combines a highly developed corporate elan with a strong civic aspect

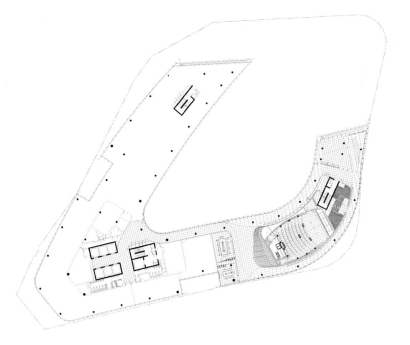

**CX 2-1,
Singapore**

1. (Previous page)
the angular prow of
the CX 2-1 recalls the
trundling Sandcrawler
fortresses of *Star Wars*
2. The horseshoe-shaped
building wraps around a
lush central courtyard.
Stepped terraces will
eventually be colonised
by layers of planting
3. The sleek street
facade tempers the
sun's glare through an
outer skin of low-iron
glass over a metallic
dot-frit inner layer

typical upper level plan

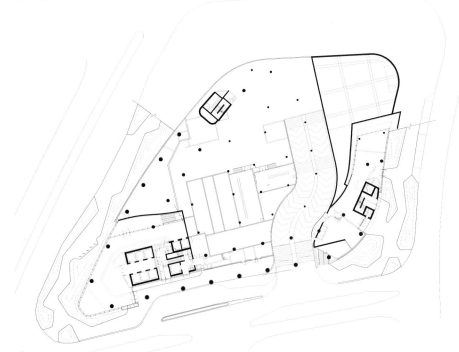

0   30m

street level plan

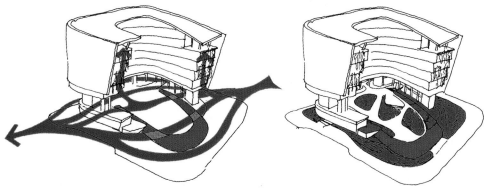

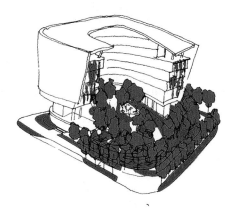

diagrams of landscaping strategy

Located near The Star and part of the same One North masterplan, the CX 2-1 building is the new regional headquarters for one of the world's leading entertainment companies. Intentionally or not, the building's sharply angular form has an evident kinship with the mobile Sandcrawler fortresses that plied the desert planet of Tatooine in George Lucas's seminal *Star Wars* film.

Perhaps more prosaically, the form arose as the logical outcome of masterplanning guidelines that dictated envelope heights and setbacks. The eight-storey building adopts a horseshoe plan enclosing lush tropical garden at its heart. At the horseshoe's ends, a series of overhanging terraces are draped with luxuriant foliage. The building is elevated on 13m-high pilotis to create a generous public space at podium level, sheltered from the sun.

This roots the structure more intimately into its setting, giving it a strong civic dimension not normally associated with corporate offices.

The original Sandcrawlers were massive, rusty and slow, but this building is impressively streamlined with a high-performance facade that addresses different contexts. From the street, the building appears delicately ephemeral, achieved through an outer skin of low-iron glass with an inner metallic-frit dot layer underneath. This enables daylight to penetrate the interior without solar heat gain. By contrast, on the lush courtyard side, the facade is more open and wrapped in a layer of highly transparent glass.

Inside, along with offices and studios, space is carved out to create an expressively contoured 100-seat theatre for screenings, performances and other events.

4. The central courtyard
will be a lush garden
5. The building is raised
on pilotis to create a
new public space, giving
a corporate facility
an unexpected and
welcoming civic dimension
6. (Opposite) detail of the
stepped terraces. In time,
greenery will cascade
down the building

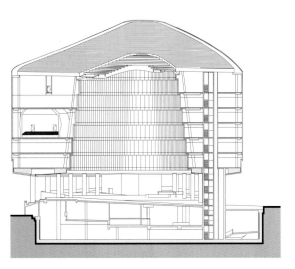

cross section

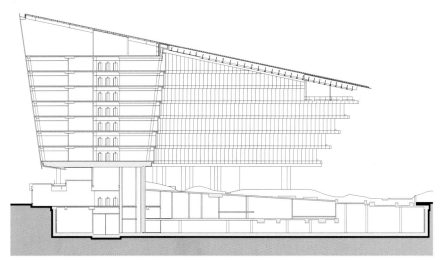

long section

TRAIN LINES

Dramatically recasting the railway station as a cathedral of transport, the Express Rail Link West Kowloon Terminus is also conceived as a new gateway to Hong Kong

Due to be completed in 2015, the Express Rail Link West Kowloon Terminus (WKT) is powerfully emblematic of the improvement in relations between Hong Kong and mainland China in recent years. Connecting Hong Kong with Beijing, the new 430,000sqm high-speed rail station will be the world's largest and most ambitious underground terminus, with 15 platforms. Intended to function more like an airport than railway station, with immigration and customs controls, the terminus is conceived as a gateway to both Hong Kong and China.

The site's prominence immediately next to the future West Kowloon Cultural District (WKCD) and Victoria Harbour demanded that the station have a strong civic quality, connecting with and enhancing the urban realm. Compounding the design challenge was the prospect of 400,000sqm of commercial development on top of the station, which will be auctioned off to a developer at a later date.

The distinctive form of the new terminal is inspired by converging forces all oriented towards Hong Kong Island, alluding to the rail tracks converging on the station itself. The station is sculpted out of the energy of these moves, opening up and focusing towards the Hong Kong skyline. Supporting spaces are compacted to allow for the creation of a large void over the departures hall and track platforms. The external ground plane is bent down to the hall and the roof structure gestures towards the harbour, making travellers aware that 'you are in Hong Kong'. Opening up towards the future WKCD, a large civic square invites people to flow into the space, encouraging them to access the station roof, which is conceived as a green oasis extending from the landscaped park below.

'The distinctive form of the new terminal is inspired by converging forces all oriented towards Hong Kong Island'

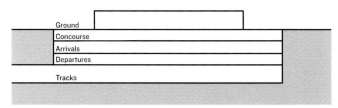

section through conventional station

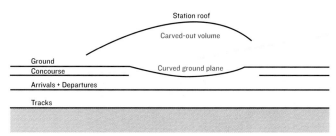

Station roof

Carved-out volume

Ground
Concourse

Curved ground plane

Arrivals + Departures

Tracks

section through West Kowloon Terminus

1. (Previous page) conceived as a gateway to Hong Kong and China, the station concourse is a soaring, luminous space that dramatically opens up to the city skyline
2. The curved and landscaped roof of the terminus acts as an extension of a new public park. The visualisation does not reflect the future West Kowloon Cultural District located adjacent to the harbour
3. An array of future top-side towers will be developed at a later date

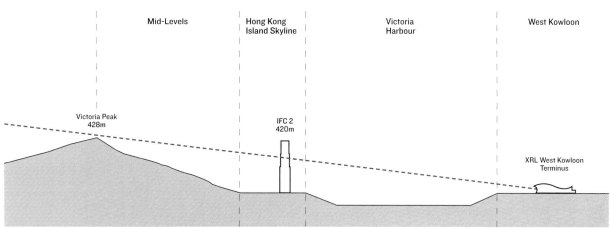

Mid-Levels | Hong Kong Island Skyline | Victoria Harbour | West Kowloon

Victoria Peak 428m

IFC 2 420m

XRL West Kowloon Terminus

site section through Kowloon and Hong Kong Island

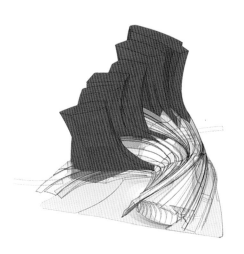

future top-side development

future top-side development

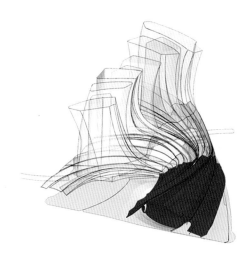

rail terminus

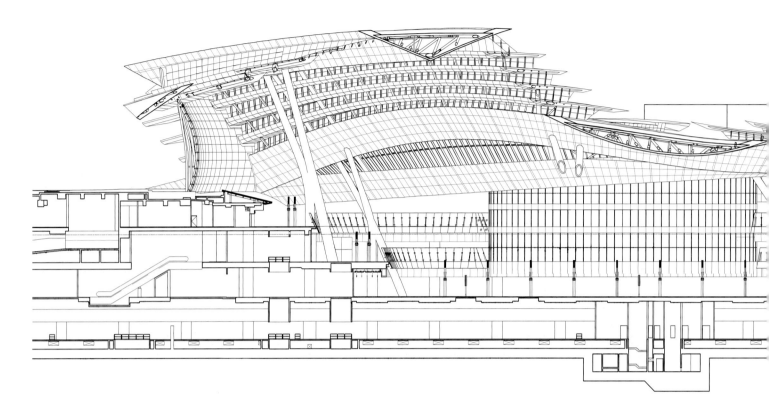

long section

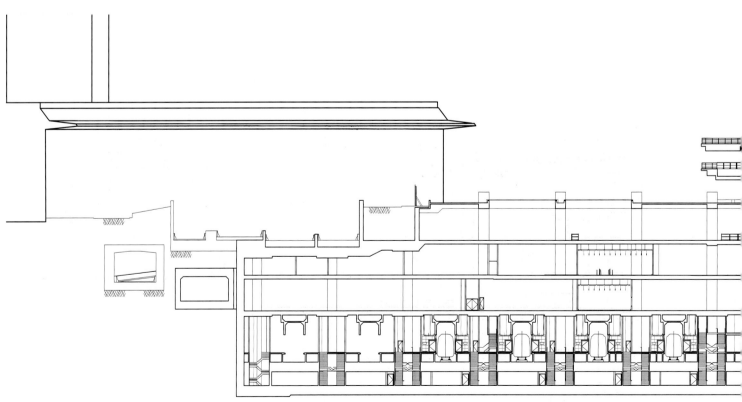

cross section

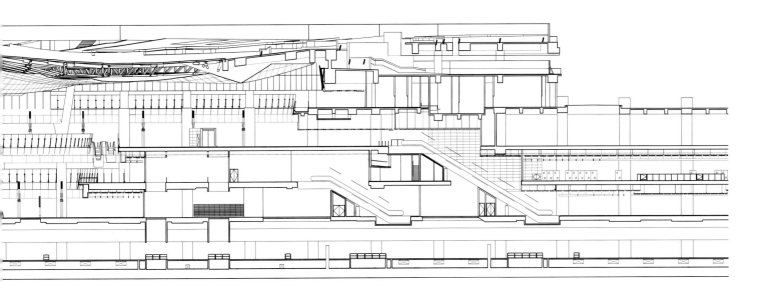

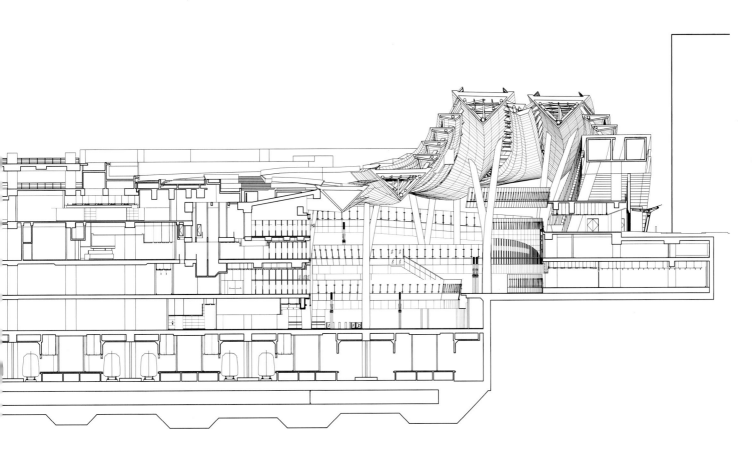

SHOW TIME

Bold forms and monumental scale give this exhibition centre in Guangzhou a powerful sense of architectural identity

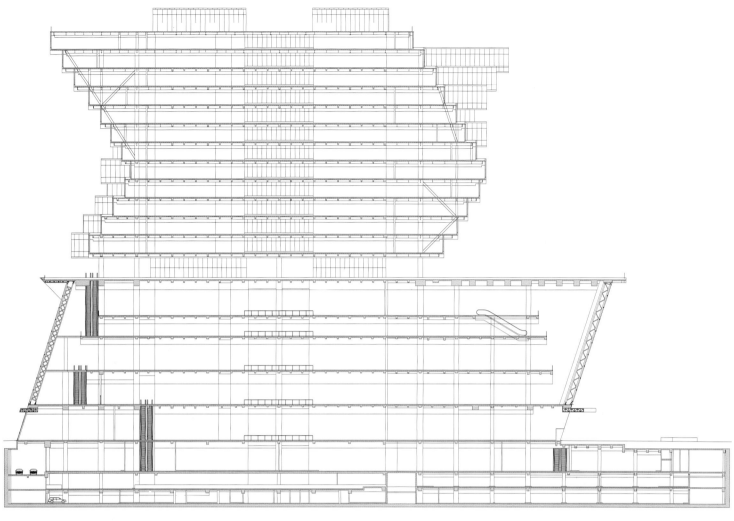

long section

Nanfung Commercial, Hospitality and Exhibition Complex, Guangzhou, China

Located on the edge of Guangzhou, Pazhou is an island in the Pearl River Delta dedicated to exhibition related activities. Pazhou's centrepiece is a huge, government-funded exhibition centre, which currently ranks as the world's second largest, providing obvious commercial competition to this new exhibition complex. This challenge was exacerbated by the fact that the two sites allocated for the new development are 160m apart and separated by a large existing building.

The introduction of four primary uses helps to diversify the new centre, creating a mixed-use vibrancy that feeds through into the business model and enhances its prospects of success. The architecture reflects this, structured around the simple concept of a podium topped by a multi-storey horizontal block. One building (1301) houses a large retail exhibition space in its podium with a large office showroom stacked on top. The other (1401) is a more conventional multi-storey exhibition centre with a 500-room luxury hotel above.

The floors of both blocks are staggered horizontally, like a very large and unevenly stacked pile of books, breaking up the massive volumes and giving the project a strong formal presence. This tactic also maximises the dialogue between the two sites, the architects likening it to static electricity leaping over the interloping middle neighbour to create a dynamic and unified sense of architectural identity. Such expressiveness is critical to how the new centre is perceived by prospective exhibitors, which serves to inform how it is marketed and ultimately its viability.

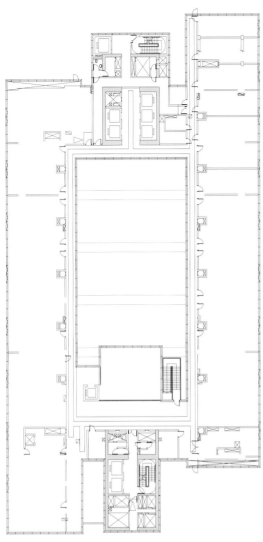

1401: plan of exhibition level

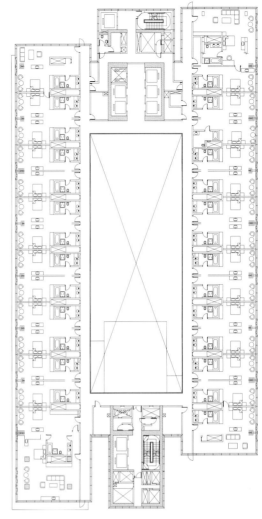

1401: plan of hotel level

0   15m

1. (Previous page) the distinctive staggered volumes of the new exhibition centre are a powerful signifier in the landscape
2. Volumes are wrapped in a sleek glass skin
3. Each of the buildings resembles a giant tottering stack of books
4. Despite being separated, the two volumes play off each other, creating a unified sense of architectural and commercial identity

'Such expressiveness is critical to how the new centre is perceived by prospective exhibitors'

DUTCH DUET

A proposal for a dance centre and school in The Hague engages performers, spectators and students in a dynamic spatial and social interplay

This unbuilt competition proposal for the Dance and Music Centre in The Hague was intended to replace the existing building by Rem Koolhaas. The project is located on the Spuiplein, an important but underused urban square in the city centre. The complex brief combines facilities for the Netherlands Dance Theatre together with its resident orchestra and the Royal Conservatory, which comprises four individual schools of music and dance. It required a clear understanding of the various performance spaces, complex circulation requirements, the way that groups can and cannot share facilities, as well the need to optimise the interface with the public. It also presented an opportunity to address the civic and social quality of the city.

All of the elements are not only formally expressed, but also consciously arranged so as to reinforce and enliven the transition from the public realm to the semi-public and semi-private zones of the performance spaces and Conservatory. The users of these facilities, audience and visitors play off each other and celebrate both differences and similarities to stimulate interaction and discovery.

The design threads a semi-public path through the building, conveying a sense of the inner workings of performance, as well as how artists develop. It establishes a framework where the unplanned and unexpected animate and inspire. Interaction between professionals and students becomes part of the building's geometry, appearing to be supportive, but from the street establishing a dramatic confrontation. In their respective rehearsal spaces, students and professionals duel across a canyon-like atrium.

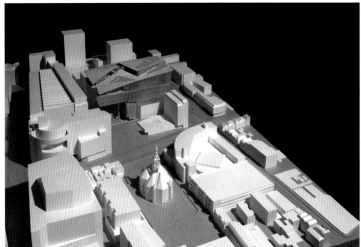

**Dance and
Music Centre,
The Hague,
The Netherlands**

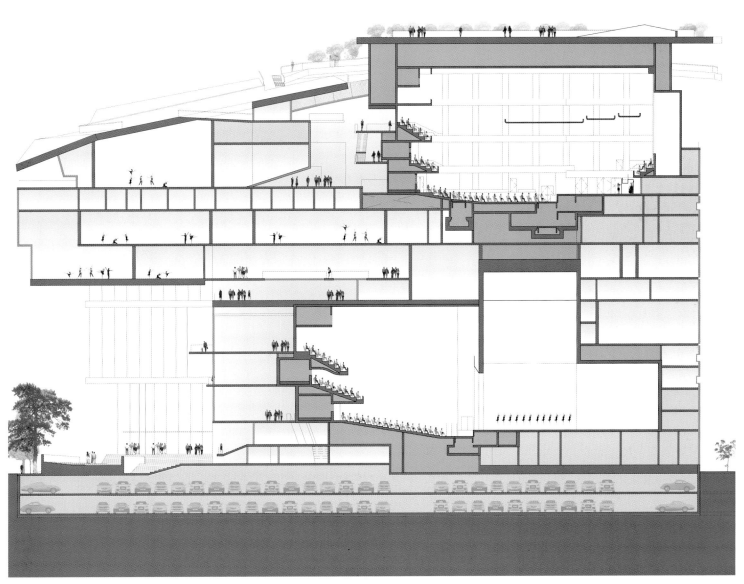

long section

PROJECT CREDITS

**THE STAR
SINGAPORE**

Client
CapitaMalls Asia Limited
Rock Productions Pte Ltd
Programme
Retail, civic, culture, cafés and
restaurants
Location
Buona Vista, Singapore
Architect
Andrew Bromberg

Project team
Tony Ang, Caroline Aviles, Jaenes
Bong, David Chan, Henry Chan,
Olivia Chan, Thomas Chan, Wayne
Chan, Grace Chen Xiao, Sam
Cheng, Sam Cho, Alvin Choo,
Allan Curr, Roderick Delgado,
Bryan Diehl, Muhammad Fadly,
Petrina Goh, Emma Hadi,
Ka-Ming Ho, Samantha Hu, Yann
Hui, Syarif Fahmi Ismail, Marcin
Klocek, Koh Thien Nee, Willie
Kua, Leo Lau, Eric Lee, Helena
Lee, Henry Leung, Francesco
Lietti, Isa Bin Lmin, Andrew
Loke, Boris Manzewski, Kenneth

Mcguire, Moreno Negri, Lancelot
Ng, Alen Nikolovski, Michael
O'Brien, Tobias Ott, Vicky Pang,
Garry Phillips, Iskandar Rahman,
Mario Sana, Eugene Seow,
Tony Sin, Joshua So, David Tan,
Tan Chai Tan, Danny Tang,
Serene Toh, Jason Wang, Lukasz
Wawrzenczyk, Ian Wigmore,
Kent Williams, Kenny Wong,
Magdaline Yeo, Ada Yuen,
Sharifah Zerdharina
Theatre and acoustics consultant
Artec Consultants Inc
Project area
62,000 square metres

EXPRESS RAIL LINK WEST KOWLOON TERMINUS HONG KONG

Programme
High-speed rail terminus, offices, retail, cafés and restaurants
Location
Kowloon, Hong Kong
Architect
Andrew Bromberg
Project team
Jaenes Bong, David Chan, Ethan Chan, Gary Chan, Katherine Chan, Tim Chan, Stephen Cheng, Crystal Cheung, Sam Cho, Winnie Cho, Alan Chong, Jason Chong, Kit Choy, Johnny Chung, Wai Chung, Adrian Geaves, Pauline Gidoin, Shawn Hau Gabrielle Ho, Mantis Hon, Samantha Hu, Stanley Hui, Yann Hui, Erica Lam, Kenny Lam, Kent Lau, Eric Lee, Grace Lee, Helena Lee, Edward Leung, Lawrence Leung, Singjoy Liang, Bonnie Liu, Jeffrey Lo, Karen Lo, Pong Lo, Kenneth Man, Frank McGoldrick, Kai Mui, Paul Mui, Louise O'Brien, Tobias Ott, Adrian Pang, Rosie Pattison, Mark Pollard, Frederico Ramos, Jeremy Richey, Malcolm Sage, David Knill Samuel, Abigail Tam, Enoch Tam, Yin Tam, Ambrose Tang, Wai Tang, Paul Tse, Kai Li Wang, Lukasz Wawrzenczyk, Richard Wilkinson, Brice Wong, Chan Wong, Dicky Wong, Jason CH Wong, Jet Wong, Samson Wong, Cora Wu, Jason Yue, Kenneth Yung
Project area
732,800 square metres

NANFUNG EXHIBITION COMPLEX GUANGZHOU

Programme
Retail, exhibition, hotel, offices
Location
Guangzhou, China
Architect
Andrew Bromberg
Project team
Catherine Behr, Geraldine Borio, Billy Chan, Henry Chan, Pong Chan, Julie Cheng, Jennifer Chik, Jason Chong, Sally Hui, Eugene Kiang, Willie Kua, Edward Lam, Helena Lee, Tiffany Leung, Katherine Luk, Alfred Mak, Tobias Ott, Maciej Setniewski, Jason So, Danny Tang, Jason Tang, Patrick Wai
Project area
288,468 square metres

CX 2-1 SINGAPORE

Programme
Offices
Location
Buona Vista, Singapore
Architect
Andrew Bromberg
Project team
Tony Ang, Darren Chan, Derrick Chan, Sam Cheng, Konrad Grabczuk, Ka-Ming Ho, Kevin Kasparek, Willie Kua, Leo Lau, Helena Lee, Kenzie Lo, Loo Soo Sing, Alen Nikolovski, David Tan, Maciej Setniewski, Tony Sin, Kent Williams, Fiona Wong, Catherine Wu, Magdaline Yeo
Project area
21,468 square metres

DANCE AND MUSIC CENTRE THE HAGUE

Programme
Theatre, education
Location
The Hague, the Netherlands
Architect
Andrew Bromberg
Project team
Billy Chan, Darren Chan, Henry Chan, Pong Chan, Pauline Gidoin, Ka-Ming Ho, Kevin Kasparek, Eugene Kiang, Willie Kua, Helena Lee, Francesco Lietti, Bonnie Liu, Vicky Pang, Maciej Setniewski, Tony Sin, Danny Tang, Jason Tang, Jason Yue
Project area
44,591 square metres

CONTRIBUTORS

Sutherland Lyall
is an architectural writer, critic and frequent
contributor to The Architectural Review.
Introducing the monograph he examines
the creative approach to practice of Andrew
Bromberg and his Aedas studio (pp4-9)

Aaron Betsky
is a critic, curator, lecturer and writer on
architecture and design. He has been director
of the Cincinnati Art Museum since 2006.
In his critique, he finds The Star creates a
new kind of public space for the dynamics
of modern spectacle (pp10-37)

Matthew Wells
is creative director of London-based
structural and civil engineers Techniker,
He appraises the complex and innovative
structural design of The Star (pp38-45)

Henry Luker
is a senior partner at engineering practice
Max Fordham. He analyses The Star's
strategy for environmental control (pp46-51)

Patrick Bingham-Hall
is an architectural photographer, editor and
author of several books on architecture in the
Asia Pacific region. He considers The Star's
Singapore context and its place in the
evolution of tropical Modernism (pp68-73)

Edmund Sumner
is an architectural photographer whose
specially commissioned images feature in
The Star's critique (pp10-37) and the informal
'Day in the Life' reportage (pp60-67)

Editor
Catherine Slessor
Designers
Heather Bowen
Asuka Sawa
Sub editors
Julia Dawson
Tom Wilkinson
Editorial co-ordinator
Phineas Harper
Editorial assistants
Manon Mollard
Michelle Sweeney
Matthew Bovingdon-Downe

Photographers
Edmund Sumner
Virgile Simon Bertrand
Marcus Oleniuk
Shinkenchiku-sha
Gerry O'Leary Photography
Patrick Bingham-Hall
Rainer Kiedrowski/Arcaid
Manfred Bortoli/Corbis
Luca Tettoni/Corbis
Pat Doyle/Corbis
Amanaimages/Corbis
Michele Falzone/Corbis
Hal Beral/Corbis
Bertrand Gardel/Corbis

Visualisations
Vyonyx Ltd
Crystal Beijing

Models
RJ Models
Tiko Models